The Ashes

Photographs and Poems

DAVID JENNINGS

RESOURCE *Publications* · Eugene, Oregon

THE ASHES
Photographs and Poems

Resource Publications
An Imprint of Wipf and Stock Publishers
199 W. 8th Ave., Suite 3
Eugene, OR 97401

www.wipfandstock.com

PAPERBACK ISBN: 979-8-3852-2833-1
HARDCOVER ISBN: 979-8-3852-2834-8
EBOOK ISBN: 979-8-3852-2835-5

08/30/24

THE ASHES

My gratitude, first and foremost, to God.

To my wife, Kristin; my daughter, Reagan; and my family and friends—thank you! I appreciate all of your love and support.

This book is dedicated to my sister, Jan.
You were simply wonderful.
I treasure the memories of our last time together at the beach.
I love and miss you.

Early morning waves wash in.
Each one sounds like a sigh
Breathed in and then breathed out again
By one who wonders why
What is must change to *what has been,*
By one who has to try
And recollect the where and when
Of some short, last goodbye.

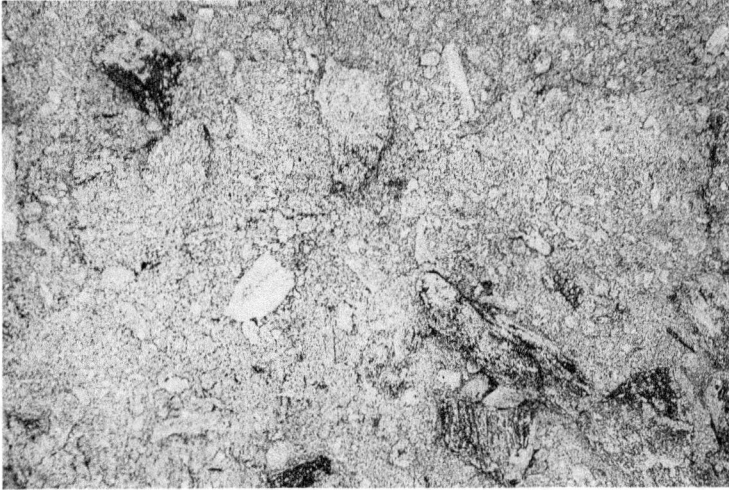

God take from me the things
For which I yearn:
My wants, my needs, my wishes
Overturn.
Strike my sins like flint
And let them burn.
Besmear on me the ashes
That I learn
To love as You have loved,
That I discern
From dust I came, to dust
I will return.

That day you put me in the dirt
Some hidden part of me was freed,
Some something of me more than seed
Began to show with sudden speed.
Shoots that had been kept inert
With water grew and stripped my shirt
And changed my in- to extrovert.

Now I wear a yellow skirt
And pose above the common weed.

Let me catch my breath—I'm
Shaking still!
I couldn't tell for sure from
That far hill
If what I saw was you or …
Yes, I knew!
I knew—somehow, I knew—that
It was you!
Two thousand seven hundred
Ninety-five,
It's you … You're here! I've found you!
You're alive!

Last summer, while the sun was warm,
I worked to make my twig tips form
Packages bound tight to hold
My hidden blooms safe from the cold.

I bore the bounding weight of snow.
I felt the ice layer form and grow
And clicked—too stiff to give and bend—
Against a raw, relentless wind.

Then came the thaw. My ice coat fell.
My tiny buds began to swell
As if they somehow knew to start
Slackening their seams apart.

As life from death at Eastertide:
Come see, my flowers have opened wide!

The secret of each pounding swell:
The truth each knows of what is veiled
Below the reach of diving bell,
Beyond the distance ships have sailed—

This truth the shore will never know,
Nor will the pausing, pensive men.
It's taken in the undertow
And hidden where it's always been.

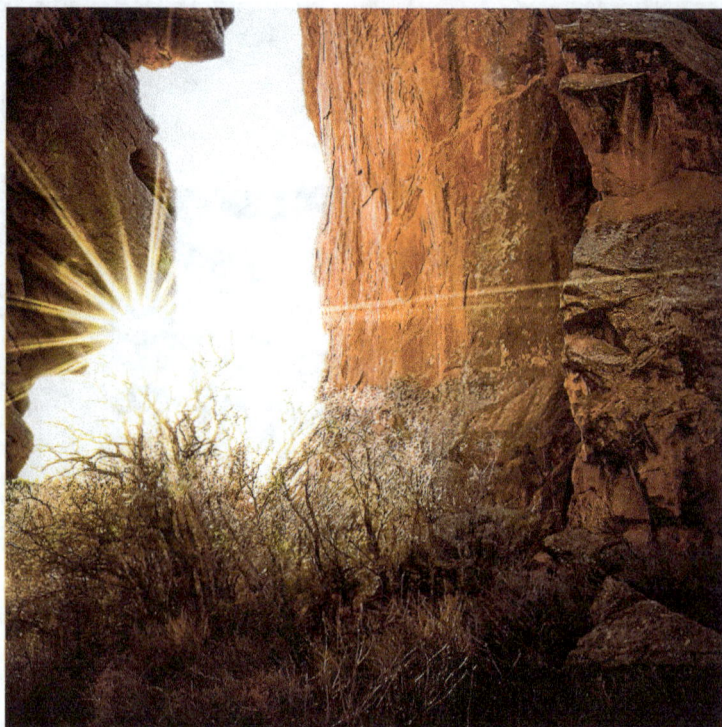

When He first called out to me
It was as if some little spark
Flickered far-off in the dark
The way a star you think you see
Glints until you look straight on—
Hints of light when all is black,
Some tiny ray through some small crack—
Then seems to fade, and then is gone.
But as the stone was rolled aside
The glow beyond my eyelids grew,
An inward breath—deep, gasping—drew.
I felt my chambered heart collide

In bounding blows against my chest.
I felt my arms and legs grow tight
As if somehow my muscles might
Move again! I turned and pressed
Up from where I had been kept
And lurched toward the blazing sun,
Letting graveclothes come undone
While Jesus and my sisters wept.

I know it seems a little odd
Comparing this to us and God
But once I've filled their hanging plate
With nuts and seeds I watch and wait
For birds to come and get their fill
(my elbows on the windowsill
And head against the window pane).

It saddens me when they abstain
From leaving roof or fence or limb,
Whistling their hungry hymn
While if they would come down their fare—
No strings attached—is waiting there.

One bird that comes can make my day.
One person—God must feel this way.

The neighbors always loathed her yard.
Please keep it nice like ours
They'd written in a scornful card
Your weeds are tall as towers!

She tore it up with disregard—
They are not weeds, they're flowers!

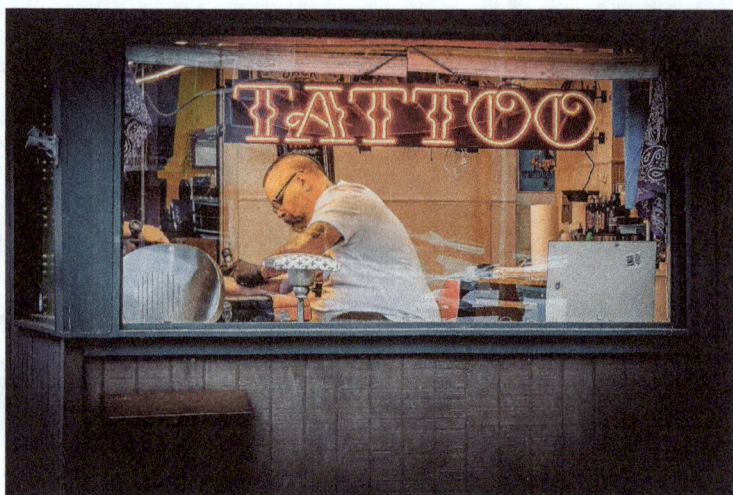

I've thought to ink my feet and hands
With four holes gouged by nails
And on my brow etch tangled strands
Of thorns—a crown—with trails
Of blood that trickles down my cheeks,
Each droplet crimson red,
And on my back show crisscrossed streaks
Like skin a whip had shred.

I've thought to mark myself to show
How He for me was slain.
I've never gone because I know
I could not stand the pain.

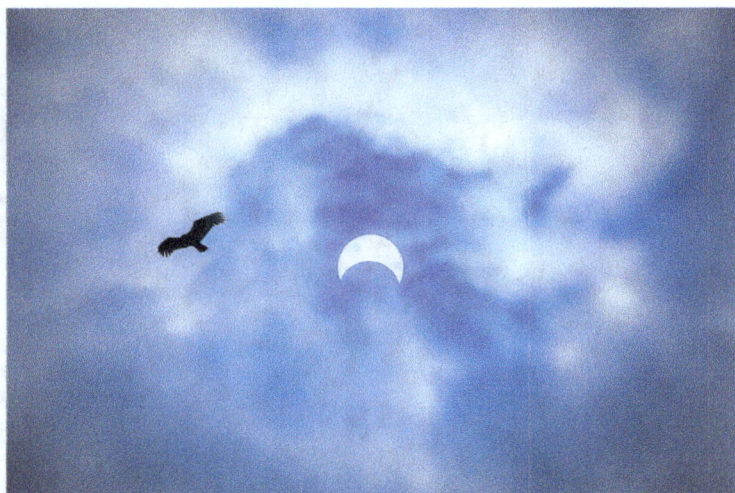

You said you'd turn the day to night.
They said the rules forbid it.

You moved as if it were your right
To face the sun and hid it.

They reveled at its rim of light
But knew you *nearly* did it!

One day I reached a branch toward you.
You did not seem to care.
OK, I thought, *I'll reach out two.*
You still were unaware.
Another and another grew
Like arms stretched in despair—
And then we touched. And then you knew.
And now we are a pair.

I think, of all the flowers, you might
Be my favorite one:
Your florets emanate like light
From a fragrant sun
And draw me from my frenzied flight
(These legs must weigh a ton!)
And tempt that I should stay the night
And leave my work undone.

Perhaps a comb
Pulled through your hair
Or plastic curlers—
Spongy, pink—
From time to time
Will take you there
And she'll be at
Her kitchen sink.

Oh, that we should never know
The fear of hearing sirens blow
That send us scrambling underground
With hands on ears to damp the sound
Of bombshells overhead.

No, pray the words are never said
Pronouncing this great country dead
Nor telling us which train to take
Nor in which camp to sleep or wake
By threat of pistol fire.

God, never that we should admire
One single sunset trapped by wire.

The poem that was left for me
Was marked in morning sand
By some gull, late from the sea,
Glad for its coastal strand.

The verse was made with metered feet,
Each letter finely traced,
But the ending—incomplete—
By waves had been erased.

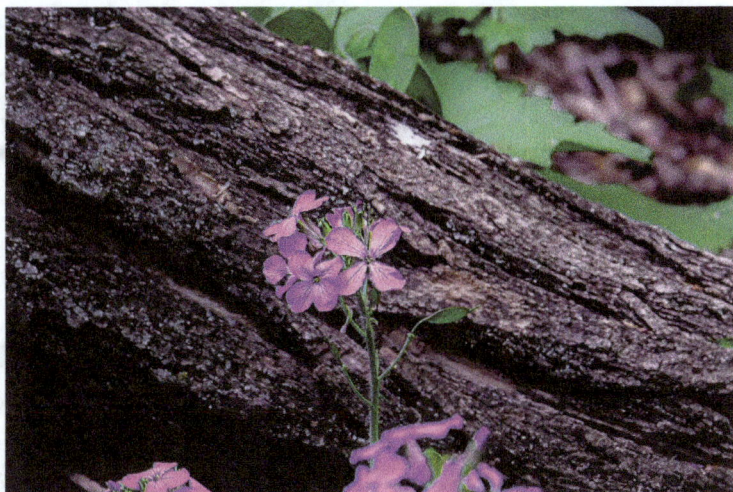

The crowd was clear which one they'd choose:
The killer, free—the Christ, accuse.
The soldiers draped a purple cloak
And crowned and struck their royal joke
Before they took Him off to die.

You take my breath—this must be why.

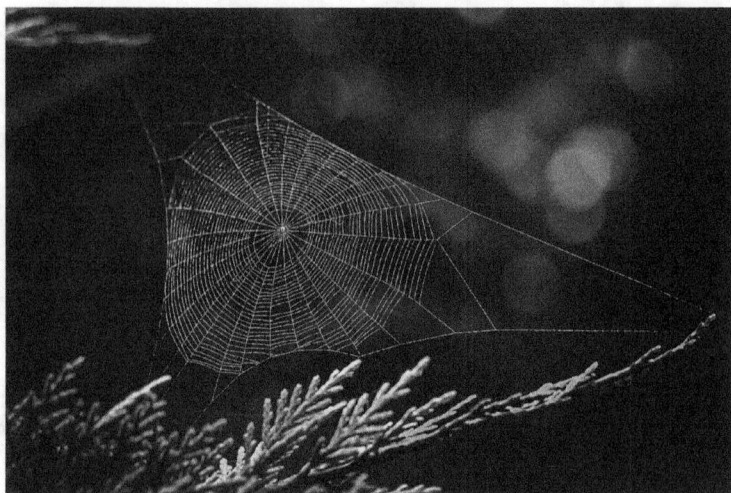

First I spin a wind-blown length
Of line that spans points A and B,
Then C and D, E, F and G
(Each betters steel in tensile strength!).
Then come the radiating spokes
Like rays emitting one by one,
The way a child will draw the sun,
That serve to act as silken yokes
Between which shorter threads are placed.
Row by row and row by row
I weave and watch my circle grow—
Each piece of string precisely spaced.

How did I come to such good sewing?
It's something I was born with knowing.

There was a different thunder, long ago:
A pounding power the prairies used to know
Of giants that would roam and lay them low
In swaths that stretched for miles—the buffalo!

Sometimes a cloudbank, in the way it's set,
Shows an image in its swelling threat:
The horns, the fur, the humps in silhouette
As if it means to say *do not forget*.

Their ancient hoofbeats storm across the sky
When lightning strikes, provoking their reply.
From echoes first, far rumblings amplify
To booming tremors as the herd roars by.

There was a different thunder, long ago:
The bounding, brawny beasts—the buffalo!

The roots that held that tree in place,
Awkward as it was—offset—
And leaning from that layered rock face
For years about to fall, were yet
Holding hard to what they could
So much so that they'd come to look
Like some poor person made of wood
Whose fingers felt for any crook
Or crevice that could give him grip
Enough that he could hold his weight
If just by that one fingertip
And not fall to some rock-strewn fate.

Perhaps one day he'll reach the top
Or let loose and that tree will drop.

I'm sorry if I startled you!
I didn't see you there.
It must have been coincidence
I stopped you in your prayer.
I only slithered out for sun,
Such darkness in the grass!
Please don't be scared—I'm not *that* one
Who caused the said impasse
Between you people and your god!
How stupid must you be
To think some snake convinced some broad
To eat from some smart tree?

Go ahead, I will stay here—
I swear to you my word.
And, once you pass, I'll disappear.
Forbidden fruit, absurd!

You've reached your branches far and wide
As if it were your leafy drive
To lend your shade to those who've died
And give relief to those alive
Who come and stand with forlorn gaze
Talking over grass and stone
In sun-scorched sweat on summer days
To someone's soul they once had known.

Or could it be your growth at heart
Has merely been to make some art?

Early morning waves wash in.
Each one sounds like a sigh
Breathed in and then breathed out again
By one who wonders why
What is must change to *what has been*,
By one who has to try
And recollect the where and when
Of some short, last goodbye.

As he'd gotten older, people talked
Behind his back: "He used to be so neat."
They'd giggle with each other as they gawked
To see him with the poor folks on the street.

His cuffs once joined together with gold chain.
His ties were silk and squeezed beneath his chin
In one tight bow that struggled to contain
His finely-pointed beard and glut of skin.

His shoes and belts were leather from Milan.
His pants were always creased. Then something changed.
One day it was as if that man were gone—
His pretense lost, his matters rearranged.

Before too long his shirts and pants were seen
On men who rummaged trash—his shoes on men
Whose job it was to sweep the sidewalks clean.
They became hearty while he became thin.

After his death, his safe was opened wide:
Not even one dropped dime was left inside.

"Stop pulling back! Stop pulling back!" His cries
Might just as well have been in some strange tongue
As nothing yelled could help me as I flung
My ballcap back and forth against the flies—
Horse flies fat as olives—where they landed,
First one then five then nine, across the rump
Of my edgy mount, sending him to jump
Up and back like one just scorched and branded
By some red-hot iron fresh from the fire!
My other hand was yanking at the reins
Which hindsight tells me logically explains
Why I nearly ended up in briar
Or underneath the hoofprint of my steed
Or bramble covered, thrown into the weed.

I know I just reflect the light
From the burning sun.
I know the case is black-and-white:
I am not the one
Who truly splits the dark of night.
Spark? Flare? I have none.

But if my tug were not so tight
Your world would come undone.

He'd always said he'd have a yacht—
At least a boat where he would spend
His later years away at sea,
And he could brag of what he'd caught
Or tell of how his pole would bend
Against the sheer enormity
Of some great fish (like Hemingway)
That fought him in some day-long brawl
Beneath a scorching, searing sun
Until the beast—with massive spray—
Would cause his line to snap and fall
As his great catch would come undone.

He'd always said he'd have a boat.
We knew the thing would never float.

Sometimes two views are so opposed
The rift cannot be fixed.
Both end up dead and decomposed,
Their red bloods intermixed
On fields where—once their clothes are stripped—
One can't tell side from side,
And neither can recite the script
For which they'd fought and died.

As brothers once, again united
Over a landscape blemished, blighted.

When you ask me where *I* was
In that condescending buzz
I hear each time that I return
(As if you think I do not earn
My namesake as a worker bee)
This time I'll gag and let you see
The nectar from my bulging crop
And shake to make the pollen drop
I've carried on my legs all day!
You eat and sleep and fly away
To woo some queen—you love-sick men—
Then drone on asking where *I've* been!

He took the silver pieces as his fee
And led them to the place where his friend prayed.
His kiss confirmed the course of history:

Besieged Messiah—Son of Man betrayed.

But when he saw his captive teacher he
Repented and gave back his wicked trade
And hanged himself from some ill-fated tree.

Can't you hear the creaking as he swayed?

I stand and watch
The waves come in.
You think I dream
Of where they've been
Or muse to know
Where they begin
Or wonder if
They'll come again.

No, I watch
The waves spread thin
And hope to see
A luring fin.

You said you'd sit and count the passing cars
When you knew that we were on our way.
Back and forth this old porch swing would sway
As cars and trucks went by until ours
Turned the corner and you'd wave and grin.

I think you'd spent more time than we could know
Out on this swing, hoping—even though
No one planned to come. I now, as you then,
Love to sit out on this swing and dream
Of things that were and times that have since passed
And long to keep these days that will not last.

As far-fetched as I know that it must seem,
Sometimes I sit and listen to the cars
And picture seeing you among the stars.

Was that You? I'd never guess
It was by how You sat:
Forlorn, defeated, lost, distressed—
Your head hung low like that.

Nor would I think to find You there
Where streets are teeming thick
With thugs and thieves who beg and swear—
The drunk, the poor, the sick.

No cloud-borne choir cried out Your name,
No angels gathered low.
I would have helped if … oh, the shame!
But how was I to know?

Little moments, here one day
Then seems a lifetime since—

Blink and they have gone away
Like shadows on a fence.

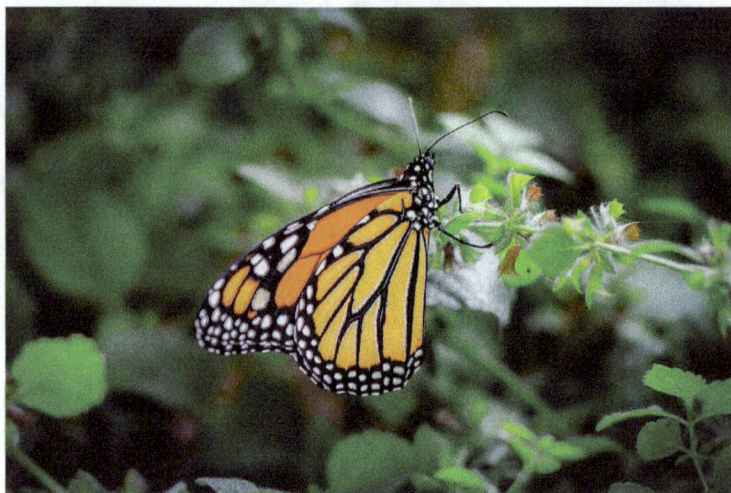

I think it's time that I should go.
I've got a duty that I owe
To folks whose folks I did not know
Who started south to dodge the snow
From somewhere north two months ago.

One by one, each domino
Has fallen in succession so
That I could fly to Mexico
And wait for warmer winds to blow
Before I flail my way back—slow—
To someone's yard or patio
In search of where the milkweeds grow.

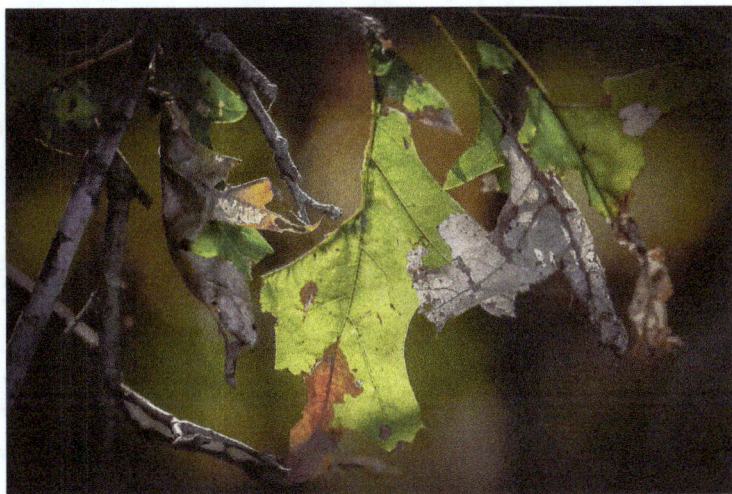

There is no way to know that it was you—
That scuffing that I heard along the street,
Like the soles of some old man's shuffling feet
Set against the cold winds as they blew
Through the window gap I'd left last night
(An inch or two to let the two cats pose
As bookends on the sill—each with its nose
Sifting scents, each tail twitching with delight).

No, I couldn't prove it you. But my heart
Hurt to hear that scraping disappear.

The last time that I saw you, you were near—
Oh, near—to having your attachment come apart
From that twig you'd held. Like a friend I've lost,
I worry it was you blown down and tossed.

That morning,
Having heard His plea
From somewhere
In that fog you'd feared,

You smiled and let
Your spirit free
And turned to Him
And disappeared.

He likened blood
To wine.
He spoke of some
Design—
A way to re-
Align
The flawed with the
Divine—
To pay a price,
A fine.

My God—the debt
Was mine.

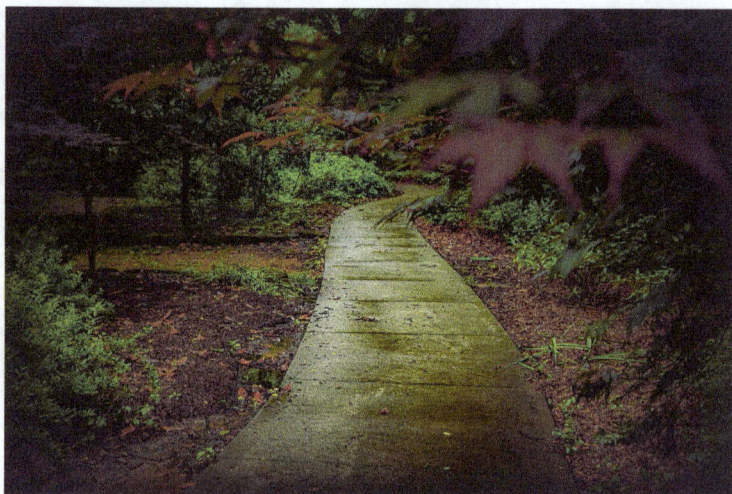

A wind gust through a window seam
Can whistle just like you.
And sleep—that sham—can craft a dream
That seems so plainly true
That when I wake I think to see
You there, but find instead
A strange uncertainty and me
Sitting up in bed.

I've not yet set the table where
I haven't held your plate
Beneath the spoon that holds your share.
I sigh and hesitate
Then put your unused plate away.

They say in time this goes.

For me, I hope that day and day
And day and day it grows
So much so that the others talk
About how sad they feel
To see me laughing when I walk:

"She thinks," they'll say, "he's real!"

I bet the rain
Is glad to find
Amongst the stones
And intertwined
Betwixt the bodies
Bound below
Roots that thirst
And sip and grow
And feed the branches
Overhead
In proof of life
Atop the dead.

I hope you know how hard I'm trying,
Sniffing at the food you're buying
And licking like I'm lured (I'm lying).
You smile and set it at my feet.
Oh Willie, please ... you've got to eat.
Who ever thought I'd turn down meat?

I try to hide how much I ache.
I know you're sad to see me shake
And hate to hear the moans I make.
Let me help—your sighed command
When you see me move to stand.
You trace my bones beneath your hand.

I am so sorry you are crying.
I love you. This must be me dying.

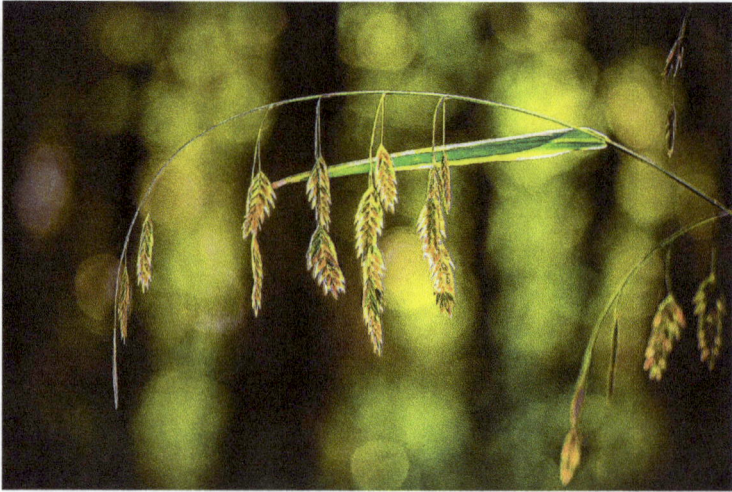

It's funny—now I stand just as you stood
And look at things I used to tease you for.
I don't mean look the way most people would.
I mean *look*, like achingly adore.
Small things that, years ago, I would have passed
(Most people do) without a second thought:
Spikelets dangling from a blade of grass,
Admiring how each little one is caught
Within the glow of autumn's morning sun.
You stood and stared and knelt to look and smiled.
I stand there staring, rapt, just as you'd done.

I get it, Dad. Now, I'm teased by *my* child!

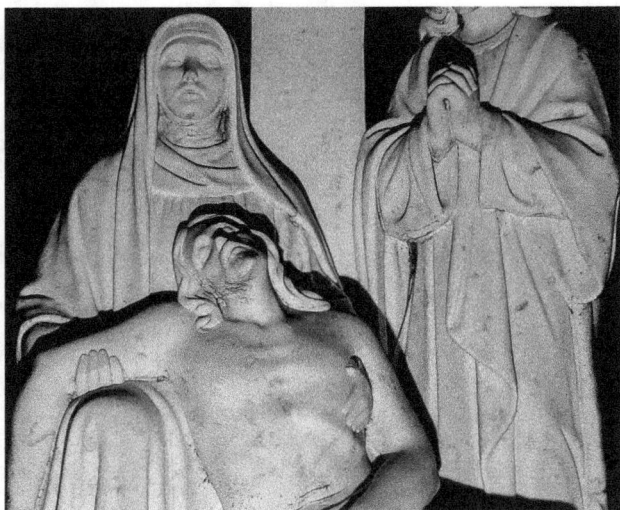

Woman, you can go away.
The ruse is over. He is dead.
Naught has come of what he'd said—
His feats, no more than pranks and play.

Weak against the gashing whip.
Stumbling coming up this hill.
All that talk was overkill—
Less miracle than showmanship.

Surely, were he what you'd thought,
He would have somehow thwarted death
Or he would gather back his breath.
But look—he never even fought.

Your *king* has died here with these thieves.
I'll bow down when he up and leaves!

I've got three of my cubs in tow.
I'm teaching them our nightly task
Of finding food. *Are we thieves?* No,
I answer to each little mask.

I've shown them how to cross the road.
They've seen the carnage cars can make:
The scattered pieces of a toad
They now equate with *one* mistake.

I've taught the terror of a gun.
They've heard how sly the fox can be.
They know the horned owl's hunt is done
In one swift plummet—silently.

I've lately taught them that a bin
Can be tipped over, spilling scraps.
Does that make a mess for men?
I've never thought ... but yes, perhaps.

My little cubs are leaving soon.
I love you, you, and you racoon.

Beneath the waves that come and go
A swift and seaward undertow
Lurks with little sign to show
As warning of its threat.

Like a clenching, knotted net
That—once entangled—will not let
Its captive free, it tugs and yet
Stays hidden from the shore.

The rip tide that you'd fought before,
That nightmare you could not ignore,
Flows deep along the ocean floor
Into the dark unknown.

Had some lifeguard's whistle blown …
But you were swimming all alone.

We cannot bring back yesterday,
Nor tomorrow see.
What use to wish the time away
On what cannot be?
Right now—right here—we have today,
But temporarily.
Look. Listen. Smell. Feel. Taste. And pray—
And pray incessantly.

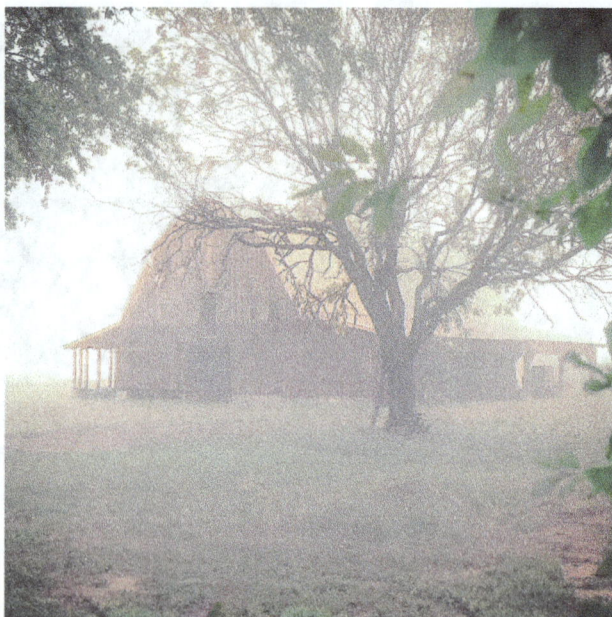

I hope my fall comes slowly on
How fall has always done,
With rain-damp nights and mists at dawn—
Wet pearls where webs are spun;

With whisps of air that loose the leaves
And send them wafting down
As remnants that a roof retrieves
To make its wilted crown.

I hope my days grow slowly brief
How autumn days are dimmed,
And I can watch, in stoic grief,
As ground and trees are trimmed

With crusted frost and dusted snow
That hint the end is near:
For me, that I in death will go,
For earth, another year.

You called out your curt inquiry:
"Who, who?" you asked. I said, "It's me."
I looked for you but could not see
Above the trunk of each dark tree.

You asked and asked repeatedly
From somewhere in the canopy:
"Who, who? Who, who?"—your anxious plea.
"It's me!" I yelled. "It's me! It's me!"

And then a whoosh—soft, feathery.

Somehow beneath the snow you knew
Where you could find a seed or two—
Remnants of the ones I threw
Hours before the storm was due.

You landed with your crest askew,
Disheveled by the winds that blew,
Then dipped your head and—white—withdrew
And looked at me, and I at you

As if … but what else could I do?

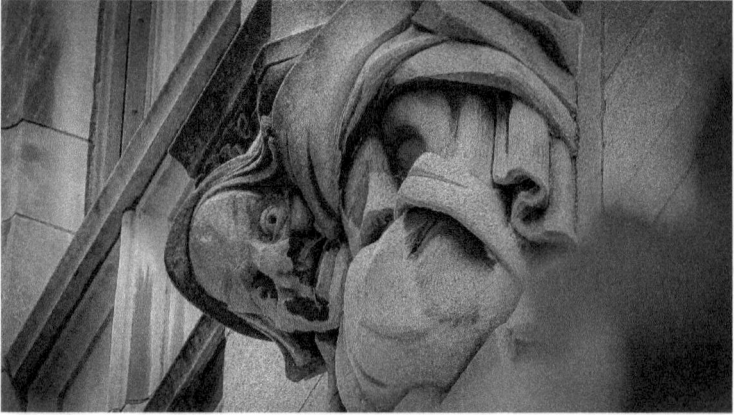

Another year grown late.
We celebrate its dying
And anxiously await
The clock strike signifying
New dreams. New hope. New date.
We drink and laugh denying
Old wounds. Old grief. Old hate.
The serpent still is lying.

Another year is great
But also terrifying.

Give me the want
That here is etched:
My knees gone weak,
My arms outstretched
And clutching where Your wrists were nailed,
My face pressed hard where Your heart failed.
Give me the yield carved on this stone:
My charge, my power overthrown
And naught but You
To fall upon.
My will, my way,
My wishes gone.
God lessen me,
Each earthly loss,
That I collapse
Against Your cross.